TABLE OF CONTENTS

ISBN 1-55035-519-8

This unit is designed as a companion piece to my earlier unit, *Classical Poetry*. Where *Classical Poetry* is useful in English courses in senior secondary school, this unit, *Traditional Poetry*, contains poems which are more appropriate for students in grades seven to ten.

Since all the poets included in the unit have been dead for some time, their works are in the public domain and can be copied without any infringement of copyright.

The unit presents biographies of many of the most important poets, a portrait of the poet, representative poems, activities and suggestions for further reading. Any of these pages may be copied by the teacher for use in his or her classroom. The portraits make excellent overheads for use in the classroom.

Students are generally interested in reading poetry, if the reading is not particularly analytical. Teachers should avoid tearing the poems apart or searching endlessly for figures of speech. Some poems may simply be read for enjoyment and brief discussion.

It is worth pointing out to students that many of the great poets of the twentieth century are songwriters and much of the music they listen to is poetry.

THE MINSTRELS OF THE MIDDLE AGES

N1-163

THE BALLAD

It's the late Middle Ages, perhaps a time during the Fifteenth Century. The townsfolk have gathered in the market place to hear a wandering minstrel sing his latest batch of ballads. They have brought their bread and their ale and look forward to a festive afternoon away from the farm or the blacksmith's shop or the mill. Television will not be invented for at least another five hundred years and so the only entertainment available is the wandering minstrel or the travelling acting company or the company of one's friends.

The ballad was a story told in song. The song was simple so that the listeners could join in, at least on the refrain. And the stories were interesting, dealing mainly with victims of human injustice.

Most of the ballads which survive today came from the late Middle Ages, a much simpler time period in which morals and values were clearly defined. So the ballads tell the stories of those whose morals are not to be admired--the unfaithful lover, the greedy person, the cold-hearted and the cruel. Ballads were composed before the invention of the printing press, so they were passed on by word of mouth and several hundred versions (with major or minor variations) exist of many ballads.

Ballads possess the characteristics of both a short story and a song. Like a short story, they deal with a simple incident, two-dimensional characters, a setting which is vague or not described and a simple, human theme. Unimportant details are omitted and left to the listener's imagination. Like a song, ballads relied on repetition or a refrain, had a simple rhythm and usually rhymed.

Most of the early ballads come from the border country of England and Scotland, and so are written in a dialect which resembles Scottish. But ballads exist from all parts of the world where people recorded their history in song--from Europe and Asia, from Africa, from Acadia, Louisiana and the Caribbean. There are even people whose hobby is ballad-collecting, who visit the elderly in remote areas of the world and record them singing the songs from their childhoods; later they transcribe the audio to print. So the ballad continues, even today, more than five hundred years after it began.

Several traditional ballads are included in this unit. Some of them are written in two versions--the first in the original dialect, the second using more contemporary language.

THE DAEMON LOVER

"O where have you been, my long, long love,
  This long seven years and more?--"
"O I'm come to seek my former vows
  Ye granted me before.--"

"O hold your tongue of your former vows,
  For they will breed sad strife;
O hold your tongue of your former vows,
  For I am become a wife."

He turned him right and round about,
  And the tear blinded his e'e:
"I wad never hae trodden on Irish ground,
  If it had not been for thee.

"I might hae had a king's daughter,
  Far, far beyond the sea;
I might hae had a king's daughter,
  Had it not been for love o' thee."

"If ye might hae had a king's daughter,
  Yersel ye had to blame;
Ye might hae taken the king's daughter,
  For ye kend that I was nane!

"If I was to leave my husband dear,
  And my two babes also,
O what have you to take me to,
  If with you I should go?"

"I hae seven ships upon the sea--
  The eighth brought me to land--
With four-and-twenty bold mariners,
  And music on every hand."

She has taken up her two little babes,
  Kissed them both cheek and chin;
"O fare ye well, my ain two babes,
  For I'll never see you again."

THE DAEMON LOVER (Continued)

She set her foot upon the ship,
    No mariners could she behold;
But the sails were of the taffeta,
    And the masts of the beaten gold.

She had not sailed a league, a league,
    A league, but barely three,
When dismal grew his countenance,
    And drumlie grew his e'e.

They had not sailed a league, a league,
    A league, but barely three,
Until she espied his cloven foot,
    And she wept right bitterly.

"O hold your tongue of your weeping," says he,
    "Of your weeping now let me be;
I will show you how the lilies grow
    On the banks of Italy!--"

"O what hills are yon, yon pleasant hills,
    That the sun shines sweetly on?"
"O yon are the hills of heaven," he said,
    "Where you will never win.--"

"O what a mountain is yon," she said,
    "All so dreary with frost and snow?"
"O yon is the mountain of hell," he cried,
    "Where you and I will go."

He struck the top-mast with his hand,
    The foremast with his knee,
And he broke that gallant ship in twain,
    And sank her in the sea.

      6

SIR PATRICK SPENS

The king sits in Dumferling toune,
Drinking the blude reid wine:
"O whar will I get guid sailor,
To sail this schip of mine?"

Up and spak an eldern knicht,
Sat at the king's richt kne:
"Sir Patrick Spens is the best sailor
That sails upon the se."

The king has written a braid letter,
And signed it wi' his hand,
And sent it to Sir Patrick Spens,
Was walking on the sand.

The first line that Sir Patrick read,
A loud lauch lauched he;
The next line that Sir Patrick read,
The teir blinded his e'e.

"O wha is this has done this deed,
This ill deed, done to me,
To send me out this time o' the year,
To sail upon the se.

"Mak haste, mak haste, my merry men all,
Our guid schip sails the morne:"
"O say na sae, my master deir,
For I fear a deadlie storme.

"Late late yestreen I saw the new moone
Wi' the auld moone in her arme,
And I fear, I fear, my master deir,
That we will cum to harme."

O our Scots nobles were richt laith
To wet their cork-healed schoone;
But lang owre a' the play were play'd,
Their hats they swam aboon.

O long, long may their ladies stand,
Wi' their fans into their hand,
Or ere they see Sir Patrick Spens
Cum sailing to the land.

O long, long may the ladies stand,
Wi' their gold combs in their hair,
Waiting for their own dear lords,
For they'll see them na mair.

Half owre, half owre to Aberdour,
It's fifty fathoms deip,
And there lies guid Sir Patrick Spens,
Wi' the Scots lords at his feet.

SIR PATRICK SPENS

The king sits in Dunfermline town,
Drinking the blood red wine:
"O where will I get good sailor,
To sail this ship of mine?"

Up and spoke an elderly knight,
Sat at the king's right knee:
"Sir Patrick Spens is the best sailor
That sails upon the sea."

The king has written a broad letter,
And signed it with his hand,
And sent it to Sir Patrick Spens,
Was walking on the sand.

The first line that Sir Patrick read,
A loud laugh laughed he;
The next line that Sir Patrick read,
The tear blinded his eye.

"O what is this has done this deed,
This ill deed, done to me,
To send me out this time of the year,
To sail upon the sea.

"Make haste, make haste, my merry men all,
Our good ship sails the morn:"
"O say no more, my master dear,
For I fear a deadly storm.

"Late late yestreen I saw the new moon
With the old moon in her arm,
And I fear, I fear, my master dear,
That we will come to harm."

O our Scots nobles were right loathe
To wet their cork-healed schoon;
But long hour after the play were played,
Their hats they swam aboon.

O long, long may their ladies stand,
With their fans into their hand,
Or ere they see Sir Patrick Spens
Come sailing to the land.

O long, long may the ladies stand,
With their gold combs in their hair,
Waiting for their own dear lords,
For they'll see them no more.

Half hour, half hour to Aberdeen,
It's fifty fathoms deep,
And there lies good Sir Patrick Spens,
With the Scots lords at his feet.

       N1-163

THE TWA CORBIES

As I was walking all alone,
I heard twa corbies making a moan;
The tane unto the t'other say,
"Whar sall we gang and dine to-day?"

"In behint yon auld fail dyke,
I wot there lies a new-slain knight;
And naebody kens that he lies there,
But his hawk, his hound, and lady fair.

"His hound is to the hunting gane,
His hawk to fetch the wild-fowl hame,
His lady's ta'en another mate,
So we may mak our dinner sweet.

"Ye'll sit on his white hause-bane,
And I'll pike out his bonny blue eyne:
Wi' ae lock o' his gowden hair,
We'll theek our nest when it grows bare.

"Mony a one for him makes moan,
But none sall ken whar he is gone;
O'er his white bones, when they are bare,
The wind sall blow for evermair."

THE TWO CROWS

As I was walking all alone,
I heard two crows making a moan;
The one unto the other say,
"Where shall we go and dine today?"

"In behind yon old fail dyke,
I know there lies a new-slain knight;
And nobody knows that he lies there,
But his hawk, his hound, and lady fair.

"His hound is to the hunting gone,
His hawk to fetch the wild-fowl home,
His lady's taken another mate,
So we may make our dinner sweet.

"You'll sit on his white collar-bone,
And I'll pick out his bonny blue eyes:
With a lock of his golden hair,
We'll feather our nest when it grows bare.

"Many a one for him makes moan,
But none shall know where he is gone;
Over his white bones, when they are bare,
The wind shall blow for evermore."

N1-163

GET UP AND BAR THE DOOR

It fell about the Martinmas time,
  And a good time it was then,
When our goodwife got puddings to make,
  And she's boiled them in the pan.

The wind saw cauld blew south and north,
  And blew into the floor;
Quoth our goodman to our goodwife,
  "Gae out and bar the door."

"My hand is in my hussyfskep,
  Goodman, as ye may see;
An' it should nae be barred this hundred year,
  It's no be barred for me."

They made a paction 'tween them twa,
  They made it firm and sure,
That the first word whae'er should speak,
  Should rise and bar the door.

Then by there came twa gentlemen,
  At twelve o'clock at night,
And they could neither see house nor hall,
  Nor coal nor candlelight.

"Now whether is this a rich man's house,
  Or whether is it a poor?"
But ne'er a word wad ane o' them speak,
  For barring o' the door.

At first they ate the white puddings,
  And then they ate the black;
Though muckle thought the goodwife to hersel'
  Yet ne'er a word she spak.

Then said the ane unto the other,
  "Here, man, tak ye my knife;
Do ye tak aff the auld man's beard,
  And I'll kiss the goodwife."

"But there's nae water in the house,
  And what shall we do then?"
"What ails ye at the pudding-broo,
  That boils into the pan?"

O up and started our goodman,
  An angry man was he:
"Will ye kiss my wife before my e'en,
  And sca'd me wi' pudding-bree?"

Then up and started our goodwife,
  Gied three skips on the floor:
"Goodman, you've spoken the foremost word!
  Get up and bar the door."

ACTIVITIES ON THE BALLAD

- 1. Ballads present simple two-dimensional characterization, which is revealed through the words and actions of the characters. Find one or two adjectives to describe the characters in each of the ballads in this unit.

- 2. Women, particularly young women, are often portrayed as victimizers in ballads. How is the woman both a victim and a villain in "The Daemon Lover"? Show that the Lady is clearly the villain in "The Twa Corbies". Read some other ballads and report on the role of women. Some suggestions are:
  - "Lord Randall"
  - "Edward"
  - "Barbara Allen"
  In each of these ballads, the woman is the villain and the man is her victim.

- 3. Country & Western music today continues many traditions of the ballad. Country songs often tell of "the woman who done him wrong" or "the man who done her wrong". Find five examples of contemporary country songs on this theme. Note any differences in the way the theme is handled today, particularly in songs where the woman is the victim. It might be useful to complete this activity in groups of four or five, so you can share your thoughts.

- 4. Each student in the class is to bring in a comic strip from a newspaper. In groups of four or five, read each comic strip. Then show that the characteristics of the ballad are found in twentieth century comics. They both have two-dimensional characters, little description of setting, a simple plot and theme. In addition, only what is important is included: Time can change from frame to frame in a comic strip, as it does in a ballad; and the background setting is often suggested rather than shown. Show how both a comic strip and a ballad are different from a movie. The *Peanuts* comic strip by Charles Schultz is a good one to use.

- 5. Use the squares on the next page to construct your own comic strip of one of the following ballads: "The Daemon Lover", "Sir Patrick Spens" or "The Twa Corbies".

- 6. Write a modern equivalent of a ballad. Choose a theme such as "love betrayed", and, if you are talented in this area, set it to music.

ACTIVITIES ON THE BALLAD (Continued)

Use the frames on this page to construct your own comic strip based on the story presented in one of the ballads you have studied.

NURSERY RHYMES

NURSERY RHYMES

Like the ballads, nursery rhymes have a long oral tradition. Many of them may date from the early centuries after the birth of Christ, but many that children know today come from the last three hundred years.

Many nursery rhymes are associated with "Mother Goose", but it is not certain if Mother Goose really existed, or if she did who she was. The grave of Elizabeth Goose (or Vergoose) is a popular tourist attraction in Boston, Massachusetts. It is said that this lady, who lived in Boston in the seventeenth century, made a collection of rhymes which she remembered from her childhood. Others dispute this claim and believe that Mother Goose may have come from France or she may be the Biblical Queen of Sheba.

Nursery rhymes seem to have been composed to make fun of political or social figures or to comment on events of historical importance. If this is so, then they are very early satires. It is quite likely that nursery rhymes at one time had meanings which may be lost to us, and so a brief look at nursery rhymes is likely to be only speculation.

That being said, let's look at a few nursery rhymes and speculate on their possible origins. Only three nursery rhymes are cited here: "Ring Around The Rosies", "Humpty Dumpty" and "Georgie Porgie". However, it would be interesting for students to research the origins of other rhymes, such as the following:

"Jack and Jill" (devaluation of the currency and fears about lesser servings of alcohol in public houses)
"Sing a Song of Sixpence"
"Mary, Mary, Quite Contrary"
"Little Jack Horner"
"Little Miss Muffet"
"Old King Cole".

NURSERY RHYMES

Ring around the Rosies

Ring around the rosies
A pocketful of posies
Husha! Husha!
We all fall down.

Many people believe that this nasty little rhyme comes from the time of the Bubonic Plague which hit Europe in the seventeenth century and devastated London in the 1660s. The plague was a flesh-destroying disease, spread by fleas which infested rats. When the rats died, the fleas fed off people.

"Rosies" were the sores caused by the plague--raised, round, red sores--and they had a ring around them. These sores often burst and a foul-smelling pus came out of them.

When the plague was in full force, people were dying faster than they could be buried, and so in plague-infested areas of London bodies were piled up in public squares waiting for burial. A person who had to travel through these public squares was often overwhelmed by the foul smell caused by the "rosies", so they carried flowers in their pockets. Once they arrived at the plague areas, they put the flowers to their noses and breathed through them, hoping that the scent of the flowers would overcome the foul smell of rotting bodies.

"Husha! Husha!" may have once been "Ashes! Ashes!" to refer to the end that comes to all of us. ("Earth to earth, dust to dust, ashes to ashes.) But it may also have been, "Atchoo! Atchoo!" since the plague caused respiratory problems.

"We all fall down" is now self-explanatory: Dead!

N1-163

NURSERY RHYMES

Humpty Dumpty

Humpty Dumpty sat on a wall.
Humpty Dumpty had a great fall.
All the King's horses and all the King's men
Couldn't put Humpty together again.

The logical explanation for this rhyme is that Humpty Dumpty refers to a fence-sitting ruler or politician who couldn't take a side in a crucial issue. His lack of decision, therefore, led to his fall, and nothing anyone could do about it could bring him back to his earlier political prominence.

However, there are scholars who believe that Humpty Dumpty did not refer to a person at all. Rather it was a very large and powerful cannon, used during the English Civil War, some time between 1642 and 1660. This cannon was placed by the followers of King Charles I in the tower of the Church of St. Mary's at the Wall in Colchester to defend the city. However, the church tower was attacked and the cannon was destroyed. Shortly afterward, King Charles I was beheaded. Thus, the King's horses (his cavalry) and the King's men could not restore him to his throne.

Still others believe that this rhyme refers to King Richard III who was defeated by Henry Tudor (later King Henry VII) at the Battle of Bosworth Field. William Shakespeare depicted Richard III as a deformed hunchback, but this was likely poetic licence on Shakespeare's part because Henry VII was, after all, the grandfather of his patron, Queen Elizabeth I. In any case, Shakespeare cites the famous line, "A horse! A horse! My kingdom for a horse!" to refer to Richard's fall from his horse. Richard was later butchered by Henry's forces. Does this mean that Richard's horse was named "Wall"?

Since Humpty Dumpty is often depicted as an egg, perhaps the rhyme only goes back to the eighteenth century. In his masterpiece, *Gulliver's Travels*, Jonathan Swift tells of a war fought over which end of a boiled egg should be cut open. Swift's reference to the egg satirizes political problems in the early eighteenth century.

NURSERY RHYMES

Georgie Porgie

Georgie Porgie, pudding and pie,
Kissed the girls and made them cry;
When the boys came out to play,
Georgie Porgie ran away.

This rhyme likely refers to King George IV (1762-1830), the son of "mad King George III", who lost the American colonies.

George IV apparently had a very wild youth: In 1785, at age 19, he secretly married a Catholic woman six years his elder. A marriage to a Catholic was forbidden to the heir to the throne. In 1787, in order to liquidate his mounting debts--caused by his extravagant life style--he allowed Parliament to declare his marriage illegal. In 1795, again to liquidate his debts, he agreed to marry his cousin, Caroline of Brunswick, but he left her after the birth of their daughter in 1796.

George IV was not popular with the English people before he became king (as regent for his insane father in 1811 and as king in his own right in 1820), and it is quite possible that he was the object of derision by the people. His immoral love life is easily satirized in the nursery rhyme.

ACTIVITIES ON NURSERY RHYMES

- 1. Research the origins of other nursery rhymes which interest you. There are several books available in the library which could be of help. In addition, the Internet is a valuable resource and contains many web pages on nursery rhymes.

- 2. Many nursery rhymes are somewhat gruesome in what they describe; "Ring Around the Rosie", for example, provides graphic details on the effects of the Great Plague. Similarly, many traditional children's stories deal with violence which parents would usually shield their children from. Read some of the original children's stories written by the Brothers Grimm or Hans Christian Andersen, such as "Cinderella" or "Hansel and Gretel". Compare these original stories with the more sanitized versions presented today in Disney movies or children's books. In groups of three or four, discuss the following question: "Should parents shield their children from the kinds of violence shown in traditional children's literature?"

- 3. In pairs, write your own nursery rhyme. Use as the subject a famous figure in politics, music or television. Try to imitate the style of any particular nursery rhyme. Read your finished rhyme to the class.

- 4. Choose a nursery rhyme character and write the name on a sheet of paper. Each student in the class then tapes the sheet of paper to the back of another student, so that each member of the class has a paper taped on the back, but does not know what the paper says. Students must then determine who they are by asking questions of each other; these questions must require only a "yes" or "no" answer.

- 5. In groups of three to five write a short play in which three to five (depending on the number of students in the group) nursery rhyme characters meet. Decide what they might talk about and what might happen to them when they meet. Present your play for the class.

PORTRAIT OF WILLIAM SHAKESPEARE

20   N1-163

WILLIAM SHAKESPEARE

William Shakespeare was born in Stratford-on-Avon in 1564. We have no record of the exact date of his birth, but it was somewhere around April 23. He died April 23, 1616, and so April 23 has become accepted as the date of his birth.

Shakespeare's father, John Shakespeare, was a tanner by trade, one who tanned hides of cattle to make leather. But John had political aspirations and was elected alderman and later mayor of Stratford. This political stature allowed Will, the eldest son and third of eight children, to achieve an education at Stratford Grammar School, a school which still exists today. Young William studied the classics, Latin and Greek, and these subjects had a great influence on his later writing; he adapted the stories to create such plays as Julius Caesar, Antony and Cleopatra and Troilus and Cressida.

When William was 18, he married Anne Hathaway, a 26-year-old spinster; six months later, their first child, a daughter, Susanna, was born. By the time Shakespeare was 21, he was the father of three children, including the twins, Hamnet and Judith. Hamnet died when he was very young, and Shakespeare apparently could not settle to married life. There are no records of Shakespeare's life in the mid to late 1580s, but we do know that Shakespeare left Stratford and went to London. Whether he left because he was trying to evade the law (some say he was accused of poaching, hunting without permission on another's property) or because he could no longer live with his wife is not known.

We do know, however, that by the early 1590s, he was an established actor living in London. Shakespeare's acting company enjoyed the patronage of Queen Elizabeth I and later King James I, and he began to write plays, not only of ancient Rome and Greece, but also of England (the history plays, such as Richard III) and Italy, the seat of the Renaissance (plays such as Romeo and Juliet, The Merchant of Venice and The Two Gentlemen of Verona). Because the reigning monarchs paid the bills, he often wrote his plays from a political stance: Cleopatra was dressed to look like Queen Elizabeth I, an obvious attempt to flatter his patroness; Macbeth ruled Scotland for 17 years of peace, but appears as a villain because Shakespeare's patron, King James I, was a descendent of Banquo, one of the men that Macbeth killed in the play. Thus, Shakespeare adapted his plots for political reasons.

Shakespeare was in his lifetime perhaps best known as an actor, then as a poet, then as a playwright. A famous love sonnet and a magic spell follow.

       N1-163

WILLIAM SHAKESPEARE: SONNET XVIII

Shall I compare thee to a summer's day?
Thou art more lovely and more temperate:
Rough winds do shake the darling buds of May,
And summer's lease hath all too short a date:
Sometimes too hot the eye of heaven shines,
And often is his gold complexion dimm'd;
And every fair from fair sometime declines,
By chance or nature's changing course untrimm'd;
But thy eternal summer shall not fade
Nor lose possession of that fair thou ow'st;
Nor shall Death brag thou wander'st in his shade,
When in eternal lines to time thou grow'st:
    So long as men can breathe or eyes can see,
    So long lives this and this gives life to thee.

WILLIAM SHAKESPEARE: THE WITCHES (MACBETH)

Thrice the brinded cat hath mew'd.
Thrice, and once the hedge-pig whin'd.
Harpier cries 'Tis time, 'tis time.'
Round about the cauldron go:
In the poison'd entrails throw;
Toad, that under cold stone
Days and nights has thirty one
Swelter'd venom sleeping got,
Boil thou first in the charmed pot.
Double, double, toil and trouble;
Fire burn, and cauldron bubble.
Fillet of a fenny snake,
In the cauldron boil and bake;
Eye of newt and toe of frog,
Wool of bat and tongue of dog,
Adder's fork and blind-worm's sting,
Lizard's leg and howlet's wing,
For a charm of powerful trouble,
Like a hell-broth boil and bubble.
Double, double, toil and trouble;
Fire burn and cauldron bubble.
Scale of dragon, tooth of wolf,
Witches' mummy, maw and gulf
Of the ravin'd salt-sea shark;
Root of hemlock, digg'd in the dark;
Liver of blaspheming Jew,
Gall of goat, and slips of yew,
Silver'd in the moon's eclipse;
Nose of Turk, and Tartar's lips;
Fingers of birth-strangled babe,
Ditch-delivered by a drab,
Make the gruel thick and slab:
And thereto a tiger's chaudron,
For the ingredients of our cauldron.
Double, double, toil and trouble,
Fire burn, and cauldron bubble.
Cool it with a baboon's blood,
Then the charm is firm and good.

ACTIVITIES ON SHAKESPEARE'S POETRY

- 1. In "Sonnet XVIII", Shakespeare asks if he should compare his love to a summer's day, but decides that she is "more lovely and more temperate". The remainder of the poem then shows how much better his lady is than a beautiful day in summer. List three major ways that Shakespeare's love is better than a summer's day. State the words or phrases which show these differences.

- 2. "Sonnet XVIII" is, of course, a sonnet. A sonnet is a poem of fourteen lines written in iambic pentameter. **Iambic pentameter** means that each line of poetry has ten syllables, written as five two-syllable pairs; in each pair, the first syllable is not stressed, but the second syllable is. The use of a regular pattern of stressed and unstressed syllables in poetry is called **rhythm**. Try this exercise on rhythm:
  - Write down the name of each person in the class.
  - Divide each name into syllables.
  - Put a slash (/) on the stressed syllables.
  - Try pronouncing the name by stressing the unstressed syllables.
  Now write any line of "Sonnet XVIII" and mark the stressed syllables.

- 3. A sonnet also usually has a **rhyme scheme**. A Shakespearean sonnet is divided into three units of four lines each, called **quatrains**, followed by two lines which rhyme, called **a rhyming couplet**. To show a rhyme scheme, we write the letter **a** at the end of the first line; all lines that rhyme with the first line are similarly marked **a**. The next line with a different rhyme is marked **b**, and all lines which rhyme with it are also marked **b**. The next different rhyme is **c**, and so on. A Shakespearean sonnet normally rhymes **abab, cdcd, efef, gg**.
  - Mark the rhyme scheme of "Sonnet XVIII". Does it conform to the pattern listed above?

- 4. Each quatrain in a sonnet usually is a subtopic of the overall theme. **Theme** refers to the underlying meaning of the poem--what the poem is really all about. The theme of "Sonnet XVIII" is the beauty of the poet's beloved, more beautiful than even a day in summer. Explain what each quatrain tells the reader to develop this theme. How is the theme summed up in the rhyming couplet?

                                       SSN1-163

- 5. The last line of "Sonnet XVIII" is: "So long lives this and this gives life to thee." The word "this" seems to refer to the poem which Shakespeare has written about his beloved. So what Shakespeare is saying is that as long as people can read this poem, his beloved will live on. Explain how the lover outlives the summer's day, but the poem outlives the lover.

- 6. You have seen so far that the rhyme scheme of a poem is related to the poem's theme. Another device which a poet uses to develop a theme is **imagery**. In order to make the reader see what the poet is talking about, the poet often creates pictures in words; these word pictures are called **images**. Three important types of images are **personification**, **simile** and **metaphor**. (Personification is discussed here; simile and metaphor are discussed in later activities on other poems.)
    - Personification is the device of giving human qualities to something which is not human. In the line, "Nor shall Death brag thou wander'st in his shade", Shakespeare personifies Death. (Note the capital letter, as if this is a name.) Death is a person who "brags" and Shakespeare uses the word "his" to refer to this non-human idea.
    - Another important personification is the Sun. Explain how each of the following lines gives a human quality to the Sun:
        - "the eye of heaven"
        - "his gold complexion".

- 7. Create your own personification. Take any non-human object and give human qualities to it. Share your ideas with your class.

- 8. Read the Witches' speech from Macbeth. Make a list of the ingredients which go into the cauldron to create the spell. Which of these ingredients do you find the most disgusting? What kind of spell might the Witches create with these disgusting ingredients?

PORTRAIT OF JOHN KEATS

26

JOHN KEATS

John Keats was born in London in 1795, the son of the owner of a livery stable. Because of his poor background, he did not study at Cambridge or Oxford, but became apprenticed at age 15 to a surgeon. He studied medicine for a short time, but devoted his life to writing poetry.

Keats's brother, Thomas, died at an early age of consumption, now known as tuberculosis. The death of his brother influenced Keats a great deal as he pondered the mysteries of a short life, noting that life is fleeting and must be enjoyed in all of its sensuous glory before it ends. This theme dominated his works. While recognizing the transience of life, Keats searched for something permanent, and this search is obvious in poems like "Ode on a Grecian Urn", in which he acknowledges the permanence of art such as the urn itself. In "Ode to a Nightingale", Keats rejoices in the sensuous appeal of nature, while recognizing that it will not last. Similarly, in "La Belle Dame Sans Merci" (called by some the most perfect poem in the English language), he regrets the passing of love which cannot last. In "Bright Star", he wishes for the permanence that stars have. And finally, in "To Autumn", he rejoices in a season of tastes, sights and sounds which will soon disappear.

Keats believed that in order to write good poetry he had to "load every rift with ore", his reference to using images and sound-producing language whenever possible. His poems represent sensuous Romanticism at its best.

Keats died of consumption in 1821. His short life produced some of the greatest poems in the English language. His friend, Percy Bysshe Shelley, wrote a poem which he dedicated to Keats. In "Adonais", Shelley wrote, "I weep for Adonais. He is dead." The next year, in 1822, Shelley tragically drowned in the Aegean Sea. Lord Byron, the third of the Second Generation Romantics, also led a short life. Ironically, all three Second Generation Romantics poets, born 20 to 25 years after Wordsworth and Coleridge, died before the First Generation poets.

Had he lived, John Keats might have become the greatest of all English poets. His brief career--only five years--attests to his potential greatness. The poem which follows, "La Belle Dame Sans Merci" has been called "the most perfect poem in the English language".

JOHN KEATS: LA BELLE DAME SANS MERCI

"O what can ail thee, knight-at-arms,
  Alone and palely loitering?
The sedge is withered from the lake,
  And no birds sing.

"O what can ail thee, knight-at-arms,
  So haggard and so woe-begone?
The squirrel's granary is full,
  And the harvest's done.

"I see a lily on thy brow
  With anguish moist and fever dew;
And on thy cheek a fading rose
  Fast withereth too."

"I met a lady in the meads,
  Full beautiful--a faery's child,
Her hair was long, her foot was light,
  And her eyes were wild.

"I made a garland for her head,
  And bracelets too, and fragrant zone;
She looked at me as she did love,
  And made sweet moan.

"I set her on my pacing steed
  And nothing else saw all day long,
For sideways would she bend, and sing
  A faery's song.

"She found me roots of relish sweet,
  And honey wild and manna dew,
And sure in language strange she said,
  'I love thee true!'

"She took me to her elfin grot,
  And there she wept and sighed full sore;
And there I shut her wild wild eyes
  With kisses four.

"And there she lullèd me asleep,
  And there I dreamed--Ah! woe betide!
The latest dream I ever dreamed
  On the cold hill's side.

"I saw pale kings and princes too,
  Pale warriors, death-pale were they all;
Who cried--'La Belle Dame sans Merci
  Hath thee in thrall!'

"I saw their starved lips in the gloam
  With horrid warning gapèd wide,
And I awoke and found me here
  On the cold hill's side.

"And this is why I sojourn here
  Alone and palely loitering,
Though the sedge is withered from the lake,
  And no birds sing."

N1-163

ACTIVITIES ON 'LA BELLE DAME SANS MERCI"

- 1. In his brief life, John Keats realized that nothing lasts forever. He searched for something permanent. In "La Belle Dame Sans Merci", the Knight, like Keats, is searching for something permanent, but he finds only a love that will not last. In order to develop his theme, Keats uses images to show that things will not last. Explain how each of the following images helps to develop the theme:"
  - "the sedge is withered from the lake"
  - "no birds sing"
  - "the squirrel's granary is full"
  - "the harvest's done"
  - "I see a lily on thy brow"
  - "a fading rose".

- 2. Sometimes an image can develop into a symbol. A **symbol** is a word or object which represents something else. A flag of a country, for example, is a symbol of that country." Both the lily and the rose can be considered symbols, because the reader will associate these flowers with other things.
  - What do the lily and the rose symbolize?
  - Why does Keats use these symbols in this poem?

- 3. Describe the image which the Knight sees in his dream in the last three stanzas of the poem.
  - Why does Keats use such a ghastly image to express his ideas?
  - How does this image contrast with the images which Keats used before the Knight fell asleep and dreamed?

- 4. Although most of the language used in this poem is familiar to all readers, Keats is trying to recreate an age of knights which is very old and so he uses some words which suggest an older form of the language. Look up the meanings of each of the following words, which suggest an older English:
  - ail
  - sedge
  - meads
  - steed
  - thrall
  - sojourn.

PORTRAIT OF HENRY WADSWORTH LONGFELLOW

       N1-163

HENRY WADSWORTH LONGFELLOW

Henry Wadsworth Longfellow was born in Portland, Maine, on February 27, 1807. Portland was a seaport and young Henry's imagination was stirred by the variety of people he met and the activity of the harbour. At school, he was a model student, whose love for reading and writing became apparent at an early age. After graduation from Bowdoin College at age 19, he travelled extensively in Europe and at age 22 he became the Chairman of the Modern Languages Department at Bowdoin. He remained at Bowdoin from 1829 to 1835 and established a reputation for himself as a great teacher who exposed his students to European literature.

In 1831, Longfellow married Mary Storer Potter, a former schoolmate, but the marriage ended in Mary's tragic death after a miscarriage while the couple were travelling in Europe in 1835. In 1843, he married Frances Appleton of Boston. Frances was killed in a fire in 1861 and Longfellow was badly burned when he tried to put out the flames. His burns made it difficult for him to shave, and portraits of him in later life show him with a long, white beard.

In 1834, Longfellow became a professor at Harvard and lived in Cambridge, where his house became a centre for learning in the university town. He published his first volume of poetry, *Voices in the Night*, in 1839; included in this volume is one of his greatest poems, "A Psalm of Life". In 1841, another volume of verse, *Ballads and Other Poems*, contained some of his most famous poetry, including "The Village Blacksmith" and "The Wreck of the Hesperus". From his friend, Nathaniel Hawthorne, he received the idea for "Evangeline", one of his favourite poems, which was published in 1847.

In 1854, he left Harvard to dedicate himself full-time to his writing. In 1855, he published "The Song of Hiawatha", a poem which caused great excitement and stirred the imagination of his readers through its Native American themes. In the ensuing years, he turned repeatedly to American history to write poems such as "The Courtship of Miles Standish" and "Paul Revere's Ride".

Longfellow remained an extremely popular poet throughout his lifetime. When it was necessary to remove the "spreading chestnut tree" which provided the inspiration for "The Village Blacksmith", the children of Cambridge donated their money to have a chair made out of the tree and given to Longfellow. After his death in 1882, a monument to Longfellow was erected in the Poets' Corner of Westminster Abbey in London, attesting to his popularity overseas as well as in America.

HENRY WADSWORTH LONGFELLOW: THE VILLAGE BLACKSMITH

Under a spreading chestnut-tree
    The village smithy stands;
The smith, a mighty man is he,
    With large and sinewy hands;
And the muscles of his brawny arms
    Are strong as iron bands.

His hair is crisp, and black, and long,
    His face is like the tan;
His brow is wet with honest sweat,
    He earns whate'er he can,
And looks the whole world in the face,
    For he owes not any man.

Week in, week out, from morn till night,
    You can hear his bellows blow;
You can hear him swing his heavy sledge,
    With measured beat and slow,
Like a sexton ringing the village bell,
    When the evening sun is low.

And children coming home from school
    Look in at the open door;
They love to see the flaming forge,
    And hear the bellows roar,
And catch the burning sparks that fly--
    Like chaff from a threshing floor.

He goes on Sunday to the church,
    And sits among his boys;
He hears the parson pray and preach,
    He hears his daughter's voice,
Singing in the village choir,
    And it makes his heart rejoice.

It sounds to him like her mother's voice,
    Singing in Paradise!
He needs must hink of her once more,
    How in the grave she lies;
And with his hard, rough hand he wipes
    A tear out of his eyes.

Toiling,--rejoicing,--sorrowing,
    Onward through life he goes;
Each morning sees some task begin,
    Each evening sees it close;
Something attempted, something done,
    Has earned a night's repose.

Thanks, thanks to thee, my worthy friend,
    For the lesson thou hast taught!
Thus at the flaming forge of life
    Our fortunes must be wrought;
Thus on its sounding anvil shaped
    Each burning deed and thought.

HENRY WADSWORTH LONGFELLOW: HIAWATHA'S CHILDHOOD

By the shores of Gitche Gumee,
By the shining Big-Sea-Water,
Stood the wigwam of Nokomis,
Daughter of the Moon, Nokomis.
Dark behind it rose the forest,
Rose the black and gloomy pine-trees,
Rose the firs with cones upon them;
Bright before it beat the water,
Beat the clear and sunny water,
Beat the shining Big-Sea-Water.

There the wrinkled old Nokomis
Nursed the little Hiawatha,
Rocked him in his linden cradle,
Bedded soft in moss and rushes,
Safely bound with reindeer sinews;
Stilled his fretful wail by saying,
"Hush! the Naked Bear will hear thee!"
Lulled him into slumber, singing,
"Ewa-yea! my little owlet!
Who is this, that lights the wigwam?
Ewa-yea! my little owlet!"

Many things Nokomis taught him
Of the stars that shine in heaven;
Showed him Ishkoodah, the comet,
Ishkoodah, with fiery tresses;
Showed the Death-Dance of the spirits,
Warriors with their plumes and war-clubs,
Flaring far away to northward
In the frosty nights of winter;
Showed the broad white road in heaven,
Pathway of the ghosts, the shadows,
Running straight across the heavens,
Crowded with the ghosts, the shadows.

HENRY WADSWORTH LONGFELLOW: HIAWATHA'S CHILDHOOD (Continued)

At the door on summer evenings,
Sat the little Hiawatha;
Heard the whispering of the pine-trees,
Heard the lapping of the waters,
Sounds of music, words of wonder,
"Minne-wawa!" said the pine-trees,
"Mudway-aushka!" said the water.

Saw the firefly Wah-wah-taysee,
Flitting through the dusk of evening,
With the twinkle of its candle
Lighting up the brakes and bushes,
And he sang the song of the children,
Sang the song Nokomis taught him:
"Wah-wah-taysee, little firefly,
Little flitting, white fire insect,
Little dancing, white fire creature,
Light me with your little candle,
Ere upon my bed I lay me,
Ere in sleep I close my eyelids!"

Saw the moon rise from the water,
Rippling, rounding from the water,
Saw the flecks and shadows on it,
Whispered, "What is that, Nokomis?"
And the good Nokomis answered:
"Once a warrior, very angry,
Seized his grandmother, and threw her;
'Tis her body that you see there."

HENRY WADSWORTH LONGFELLOW: HIAWATHA'S CHILDHOOD (Continued)

Saw the rainbow in the heaven,
In the eastern sky the rainbow,
Whispered, "What is that, Nokomis?"
And the good Nokomis answered:
"'Tis the heaven of flowers you see there:
All the wildflowers of the forest,
All the lilies of the prairie,
When on earth they fade and perish,
Blossom in that heaven above us."

When he heard the owls at midnight,
Hooting, laughing in the forest,
"What is that?" he cried in terror;
"What is that," he said, "Nokomis?"
And the good Nokomis answered:
"That is but the owl and owlet,
Talking in their native language,
Talking, scolding at each other."

Then the little Hiawatha
Learned of every bird its language,
Learned their names and all their secrets,
How they built their nests in summer,
Where they hid themselves in winter,
Talked with them whene'er he met them,
Called them "Hiawatha's Chickens."

Of all beasts he learned the language,
How the beavers built their lodges,
Where the squirrels hid their acorns,
How the reindeer ran so swiftly,
Why the rabbit was so timid,
Talked with them whene'er he met them,
Called them "Hiawatha's Brothers."

ACTIVITIES ON "THE VILLAGE BLACKSMITH"

- 1. In "The Village Blacksmith", Longfellow paints a picture of one aspect of life in Cambridge, Massachusetts, then a small town or perhaps even a village, even though it was the site of Harvard University. Even in his own time, life was changing rapidly, and the village blacksmith represents some of the old, traditional values. The language of the poem may seem strange to modern readers, although much of it would have been instantly recognizable in Longfellow's time. Look up the meaning of each of the following words:
  - sinewy, brawny
  - bellows, sledge, forge, anvil, wrought
  - sexton
  - chaff
  - threshing
  - toiling.

- 2. Another figure of speech which presents an image is a **simile**. A simile is a direct comparison between two unlike things. It is easy to spot a simile because it always uses the words "like" or "as". "And the muscles on his brawny arms/Are strong as iron bands" is a simile. The blacksmith's muscles are being compared to iron bands. Iron bands and muscles are unlike things, but they do have something in common, and therefore the simile works. What do the blacksmith's muscles have in common with iron bands?
Longfellow again uses the word "like" to compare his daughter's voice to her mother's voice, but this is not a simile because he is comparing two similar things (two voices), not two unlike things. However, there are at least two other real similes in this poem. Find each one, state what two unlike things are being compared, and explain what they have in common.

- 3. A **metaphor** is also a comparison between two unlike things, but it does not use the words "like" or "as". So, a metaphor is called an implied comparison because the comparing words ("like", "as") are not directly stated. A metaphor says that one thing *is* another. "The muscles of the blacksmith's arms are iron bands" would be a metaphor; "the muscles are like iron bands" would be a simile. In the last stanza of the poem, Longfellow uses a metaphor: "At the flaming forge of life/Our fortunes must be wrought." This metaphor compares life with the blacksmith's forge--and this is how we learn the lesson which the poet refers to in the last stanza. Explain how life is like the blacksmith's forge.

ACTIVITIES ON "HIAWATHA'S CHILDHOOD"

- 1. Longfellow's story of Hiawatha is one of the most famous in American literature. It is set "by the shores of Gitche Gumee", the Indian name for Lake Superior, the "shining Big-Sea-Water". However, the poem has come under attack in recent years because it appears to depict a stereotypical portrait of the North American Indian. Defend the poem against its critics by pointing out examples of the nobility of the native peoples which Longfellow shows in the poem. What examples can you find which perpetuate the stereotype of the North American Indian?

- 2. Look up the meaning of each of the following words:
  - linden
  - sinews
  - fretful
  - tresses
  - lapping
  - lodges
  - timid.

- 3. The native peoples respected the animals for their ability to adapt to their environment and survive in the wilderness. Find two examples of this respect for animals. For each example, show what all people may learn.

- 4. Longfellow uses very few figures of speech (simile, metaphor, personification) in this poem, yet he creates a very vivid picture of the environment which influences Hiawatha's early life. Draw a picture of this environment, including as many natural objects as you can.

- 5. Longfellow chooses his words and arranges them to create a rhythm in this poem.
  - Words with long vowel sounds tend to slow down the rhythm; words with short vowel sounds speed it up. Find examples of words with both long and short vowel sounds in the first two stanzas of the poem. How many long sounds are there in comparison with short sounds?
  - How would you describe the rhythm of this poem? Does it sound like anything with which you are familiar?

PORTRAIT OF ALFRED LORD TENNYSON

38

ALFRED LORD TENNYSON

If John Keats had been allowed to live longer, he might have written the kind of poetry which Alfred Lord Tennyson wrote. To put this another way, if Keats had written both his own poetry and the early poetry of Tennyson, he might have become the greatest poet in the English language. Tennyson, however, did not profess any allegiance to Keats; instead he professed to an admiration of the poetry of Lord Byron, another of the great Second Generation Romantic poets.

Tennyson was born in 1809, in Somersby, Lincolnshire, England, the son of a clergyman. Like many of the great poets, he was educated at Cambridge, where he won awards for his writing. He became a very close of Arthur Hallam and served with Hallam in the Spanish revolutionary army against King Ferdinand VII's despotic rule. In 1832, he published several of his poems, including "The Lady of Shalott" and "The Lotos-Eaters". This anthology of poems received poor critical reviews; however, the anthology contains poems which today are considered masterpieces.

The next year, 1833, Hallam died suddenly. Hallam's death so profoundly influenced Tennyson that he refused to publish poetry for ten years, although he did continue to write during this period. In 1842, the publication of a two-volume set of his poems, which included "Ulysses", "Morte d'Arthur", "Locksley Hall" and "Break, Break, Break", won critical acclaim and established Tennyson as the foremost English poet of his time. In 1850, he published *In Memoriam*, another anthology of poems, this one dedicated to the memory of Arthur Hallam. In the same year, he was made poet-laureate of England on the death of William Wordsworth. As poet-laureate, he wrote poems to celebrate British achievements and losses, such as "The Charge of the Light Brigade". Also in 1850, Tennyson married Emily Sellwood and lived on the Isle of Wight for some time each year for the remainder of his life.

Tennyson later published *Idylls of the King*, a series of poems about King Arthur. However, much of his later writing tended to be conservative, restrained and somewhat dull. He was made a baron (hence, the *Lord* in Alfred *Lord* Tennyson) in 1884 and died in 1892.

Tennyson's poetry more than that of any other writer embodies the Victorian age. More importantly, his verse is beautiful to read for the rhythms and the sounds of his words. He is truly a great English poet.

ALFRED LORD TENNYSON: THE CHARGE OF THE LIGHT BRIGADE

Half a league, half a league,
Half a league onward,
All in the valley of Death
   Rode the six hundred.
"Forward, the Light Brigade!
Charge for the guns!" he said:
Into the valley of Death
   Rode the six hundred.

"Forward, the Light Brigade!"
Was there a man dismayed?
Not though the soldier knew
   Someone had blundered:
Theirs not to make reply,
Theirs not to reason why,
Theirs but to do and die:
Into the valley of Death
   Rode the six hundred.

Cannon to right of them,
Cannon to left of them,
Cannon in front of them
   Volleyed and thundered;
Stormed at with shot and shell,
Boldly they rode and well,
Into the jaws of Death,
Into the mouth of Hell
   Rode the six hundred.

Flashed all their sabres bare,
Flashed as they turned in air
Sabring the gunners there,
Charging an army, while
   All the world wondered:
Plunged in the battery-smoke
Right through the line they broke;
Cossack and Russian
Reeled from the sabre-stroke,
   Shattered and sundered.
Then they rode back, but not,
   Not the six hundred.

Cannon to right of them,
Cannon to left of them,
Cannon behind them
   Volleyed and thundered:
Stormed at with shot and shell,
While horse and hero fell,
They that had fought so well
Back from the mouth of Hell,
All that was left of them,
   Left of six hundred.

When can their glory fade?
O the wild charge they made!
   All the world wondered.
Honour the charge they made!
Honour the Light Brigade,
   Noble six hundred!

ACTIVITIES ON "THE CHARGE OF THE LIGHT BRIGADE"

- 1. Alfred Lord Tennyson became poet laureate of Great Britain in 1850. His job was to write poetry in praise of the country and the British Empire. By 1853, Britain was involved in the Crimean War, between Turkey and the Russian Empire. Allied with France and Sardinia, Britain supported the Turks in this war staged in what is today the Ukraine. On October 25, 1854, the Russians met the British at Balaclava (also spelled *Balaklava*). Because of a misunderstood order, the Light Brigade charged into the valley in one of the worst disasters of the War for the British. This bungled attack received very poor press in Britain, and so Tennyson wrote the poem in order to bring honour and praise to what many believed was a shameful disgrace. Choose three phrases from the poem which honour the Light Brigade and explain why these phrases are appropriate.

- 2. Look up the meaning of each of the following words:
  - league (meaning a distance)
  - dismayed
  - blundered
  - volleyed
  - sabre
  - Cossack.

- 3. The second stanza tells of the soldiers' response to the misunderstood orders. Why is not only appropriate, but also necessary, for soldiers to react in the way stated?

- 4. Find two examples of personification in this poem. Explain why each example is appropriate.

- 5. More British soldiers died of starvation and cholera than were killed by the Russians during the Crimean War. One of the great heroes of the War was Florence Nightingale, the "Lady with the Lamp". Research the life of Florence Nightingale to learn her great contributions to the world.

- 6. Write a story or a poem about a great hero, a real person whom you admire. In what ways is your hero like the soldier of the Light Brigade or like Florence Nightingale?

PORTRAIT OF SIR WALTER SCOTT

SIR WALTER SCOTT

Sir Walter Scott was born in Edinburgh, Scotland, in 1771, and trained as a lawyer. He became a lawyer at the age of 21 in 1792 and worked at law throughout his life. However, it was not as a lawyer that he made his fame, but as a novelist, poet, translator, and critic--in short, as one of the most famous literary figures of his time.

Scott loved the old legends, and these have inspired many of his stories. His love of mediaeval ballads led to the publication of *The Ministrelsy of the Scottish Border*, an edition of ballads, in 1803. In 1805, his first narrative poem, "The Lay of the Last Minstrel", made him extremely popular. Later narrative poems include "Marmion", "The Lady of the Lake", "The Lord of the Isles" and "Lochinvar", which is used in this unit. When he turned to writing novels, Scott again looked to the old legends. Among his most popular novels are *Ivanhoe*, *Rob Roy*, *The Bride of Lammermoor*, *Quentin Durward*, *The Heart of Midlothian*, and *Kenilworth*.

In 1820, Scott was made a baronet, the first person to gain this honour solely for literary achievements, and built a mansion called *Abbotsford*. Although he made a great deal of money as a writer, he became involved in legal entanglements with printers and publishers, and spent the rest of his life attempting to repay his debts. He died at Abbotsford in 1832.

Sir Walter Scott is probably the first major historical novelist. His stories are often written on an epic scale, and many have been made into movies. He brought about a new interest in Scottish history and traditions which spread around the world and has remained until today. Finally, his influence on other writers can be seen in the works of James Fenimore Cooper in the United States, Honoré de Balzac in France, and Charles Dickens in England.

SIR WALTER SCOTT: LOCHINVAR

O, young Lochinvar is come out of the west,
Through all the wide Border his steed was the best;
And, save his good broadsword, he weapon had none,
He rode all unarmed, and he rode all alone.
So faithful in love, and so dauntless in war,
There never was knight like the young Lochinvar.

He stayed not for brake, and he stopped not for stone,
He swam the Eske river where ford there was none;
But, ere he alighted at Netherby gate,
The bride had consented, the gallant came late;
For a laggard in love, and a dastard in war,
Was to wed the fair Ellen of brave Lochinvar.

So boldly he entered the Netherby Hall,
Among bridesmen, and kinsmen, and brothers, and all.
Then spoke the bride's father, his hand on his sword,
(For the poor craven bridegroom said never a word),
"O come ye in peace here, or come ye in war,
Or to dance at our bridal, young Lord Lochinvar?"

"I long wooed your daughter, my suit you denied;--
Love swells like the Solway, but ebbs like its tide,--
And now am I come, with this lost love of mine,
To lead but one measure, drink one cup of wine.
There are maidens in Scotland more lovely by far,
That would gladly be bride to the young Lochinvar."

The bride kissed the goblet; the knight took it up,
He quaffed off the wine, and he threw down the cup.
She looked down to blush, and she looked up to sigh,
With a smile on her lips, and a tear in her eye.
He took her soft hand, ere her mother could bar,--
"Now tread we a measure!" said young Lochinvar.

So stately his form, and so lovely her face,
That never a hall such a galliard did grace;
While her mother did fret, and her father did fume,
And the bridegroom stood dangling his bonnet and plume;
And the bride-maidens whispered, "'Twere better by far,
To have matched our fair cousin with young Lochinvar."

One touch to her hand, and one word in her ear,
When they reached the hall-door and the charger stood near
So light to the croup the fair lady he swung,
So light to the saddle before her he sprung!
"She is won! we are gone! over bank, bush, and scaur;
They'll have fleet steeds that follow," quoth young Lochinvar.

There was mounting 'mong Graemes of the Netherby clan;
Forsters, Fenwicks, and Musgraves, they rode and they ran;
There was racing and chasing on Cannobie Lee,
But the lost bride of Netherby ne'er did they see.
So daring in love and so dauntless in war,
Have ye e'er heard of gallant like young Lochinvar?

ACTIVITIES ON "LOCHINVAR"

- 1. Notice the unusual rhythm of this poem. Each line consists of eleven syllables, set up as four feet. Remember that a foot is a rhyming pattern. The first foot in each line consists of an unaccented syllable followed by an accented syllable. The next three feet each consist of two unaccented syllables followed by an accented syllable. Thus, each line has a rhythm of *de-dum, de-de-dum, de-de-dum, de-de-dum*, with the accents falling on the dum. Read each line out loud, emphasizing the accents. Do they sound like horses' hooves? Why is this rhythm appropriate to the content of the poem?

- 2. Look up the meaning of each of the following words:
  - dauntless
  - brake (a word from Scottish dialect, not the mechanism for stopping a car)
  - alighted
  - laggard
  - dastard
  - craven
  - quaffed
  - galliard
  - croup.

- 3. Scott has purposely chosen old words which are seldom seen today in the language. These old, no-longer-used words are called **archaic words**. Find examples of three or four archaic words in the poem, and explain why each one is appropriate to the theme and setting of the poem.

- 4. Notice that Scott has imitated the medieval ballad in writing this poem. Explain how the characterization and description of the setting imitate the medieval ballad.

- 5.Write a ballad rap. Imitate the style of today's rap music to write a ballad which tells a story. If you wish, you may use a knight as your central character. You may write this assignment in groups of three or four and then present your ballad rap orally to the class.

PORTRAIT OF EDWARD LEAR

EDWARD LEAR

The well-known humorist and artist, Edward Lear, was born in London, England, in 1812, and began a career at age 19 as a painter of animals and birds for the London Zoological Society. He gained an early reputation for his paintings of birds in the 1832 book, *The Family of the Psittacidae*. Lord Stanley commissioned Lear to draw the animals in his private zoo, and during his five years in Lord Stanley's house, he began to write and illustrate nonsense rhymes and limericks for Lord Stanley's children.

In 1846, Lear published *A Book of Nonsense*, which enjoyed such enormous popularity that he published several more books of nonsense poetry. These include *Nonsense Songs, Stories, Botany and Alphabets* in 1871, the volume which includes "The Owl and the Pussycat".

Lear travelled extensively throughout Europe and the Middle East, before settling in San Remo, Italy in 1870. In his travels, he drew pictures of landscapes and buildings and made notes of his experiences. These became the basis of *The Illustrated Journals of a Landscape Painter*. Lear died in San Remo in 1880.

Although Edward Lear was an exceptional painter, he is now considered to be the master of nonsense poetry, especially the **limerick**, which he popularized in his verse. A limerick is a five line piece of poetry, which rhymes aabba. It often begins with a line such as "There was a young [or an old] man [or woman, or boy, or girl, etc.] from [name of place]." His poems, such as "The Old and the Pussycat", are seen by some as pure nonsense and fun; others see great meaning in the poems. Often the reader's response to the poetry of Edward Lear appears to be more important than the lyrics themselves.

Teachers should emphasize the fun aspects of Lear's poetry, but make room also for students to respond personally to the poems.

                                       N1-163

EDWARD LEAR: THE OWL AND THE PUSSY-CAT

The Owl and the Pussy-cat went to sea
  In a beautiful pea-green boat:
They took some honey, and plenty of money
  Wrapped up in a five-pound note.
The Owl looked up to the stars above,
  And sang to a small guitar,
"O lovely Pussy, O Pussy, my love,
  What a beautiful Pussy you are,
      You are,
      You are!
  What a beautiful Pussy you are.

Pussy said to the Owl, "You elegant fowl,
  How charmingly sweet you sing!
Oh! let us be married; too long we have tarried:
  But what shall we do for a ring?"
They sailed away, for a year and a day,
  To the land where the bong-tree grows;
And there in a wood a Piggy-wig stood,
  With a ring at the end of his nose,
      His nose,
      His nose,
  With a ring at the end of his nose.

"Dear Pig, are you willing to sell for one shilling
  Your ring?" Said the Piggy, "I will."
So they took it away, and were married next day
  By the turkey who lives on the hill.
They dined on mince and slices of quince,
  Which they ate with a runcible spoon;
And hand in hand, on the edge of the sand,
  They danced by the light of the moon,
      The moon,
      The moon,
  They danced by the light of the moon.

ACTIVITIES ON "THE OWL AND THE PUSSYCAT"

- 1. Like "Lochinvar", this poem also has an unusual rhythm. Much of this rhythm is enhanced by words in the middle of a line which rhyme with words at the end of the line. Find three examples of words in the middle of the line which rhyme with words at the end of the line.

- 2. A "runcible spoon" is a term which we rarely use. It is, in fact, not a spoon at all, but a fork with two wide prongs and a sharp-edged curved prong. Similarly, "bong-tree" may be a word which Lear made up; it may be related to *billabong*, which in Australia means a *lagoon*. Look up the meaning of each of the following words:
  - tarried
  - shilling (and five-pound note)
  - mince (think of *minced meat* or *minced tarts*)
  - quince.

- 3. Write your own nonsense poem, imitating the style used by Edward Lear in "The Owl and the Pussycat". If you wish, you may write a poem about two unusual creatures who fall in love. Also, you may decide to make up some words of your own to use in the poem.

- 4. Compose your own limerick. Remember that a limerick contains five lines which rhyme *aabba*. Start with the line: *There was a young [or old] person [man, woman, boy, girl] from [name of place].* Share your limerick by reciting it to the class.

- 5. Lear called his poems *nonsense poetry*. Do you think that "The Owl and the Pussycat" is pure nonsense and fun, or does it have a deeper meaning? Discuss this question in groups of three or four and try to arrive at consensus. Be sure that you are able to support your view with references from the poem.

PORTRAIT OF WALT WHITMAN

N1-163

WALT WHITMAN

Born of a poor Quaker family on a farm on Long Island, New York in 1819, Walt Whitman worked at a variety of jobs including office boy, itinerant schoolteacher and carpenter, before becoming a journalist in Brooklyn and New Orleans. In 1855, Whitman published a volume of twelve poems entitled Leaves of Grass, a volume which he was to revise for his entire life. The final version of the book, published just before his death, was much longer.

During the American Civil War, he worked as a nurse in army hospitals in Washington and Virginia. After the war, he became a civil servant, but he continued to write his poetry.

In 1873, he suffered the first of a series of paralytic strokes and moved to Camden, New Jersey, where he spent the remainder of his life. In his later years, his home in Camden was often visited by his many admirers from both the United States and other countries. He died there in 1892 and is buried in Camden in a tomb which he designed himself. His home is now a museum, dedicated to his works.

While writers such as Hawthorne and Poe concerned themselves with the pessimistic themes of evil and death, Whitman celebrated life, the dignity of the common man, and the ideal of universal brotherhood. His work was greatly admired and supported by other American writers, such as Henry David Thoreau and Ralph Waldo Emerson, and many twentieth century poets cite Whitman as a major influence.

His most famous poems are two elegies written in memory of President Abraham Lincoln: "When Lilacs Last in the Dooryard Bloomed" is perhaps his greatest work; "O Captain! My Captain!" is undoubtedly his most popular poem. Both were published in 1866 in a book of poems called Sequel.

WALT WHITMAN: A NOISELESS PATIENT SPIDER

A noiseless, patient spider
I mark'd, where, on a little promontory, it stood, isolated;
Mark'd how, to explore the vacant, vast surrounding,
It launch'd forth filament, filament, filament, out of itself;
Ever unreeling them, ever tirelessly speeding them.

And you, O my Soul, where you stand,
Surrounded, detached, in the measureless oceans of space,
Ceaselessly musing, venturing, throwing,--seeking the spheres,
    to connect them;
Till the bridge you will need, be form'd, till the ductile anchor hold;
Till the gossamer thread you fling, catch somewhere, O my Soul.

ACTIVITIES ON "A NOISELESS PATIENT SPIDER"

- 1. Look up the meaning of each of the following words:
  - mark'd (or marked)
  - promontory
  - isolated
  - vacant
  - filament
  - detached
  - ceaselessly
  - musing
  - venturing
  - ductile
  - gossamer.

- 2. The story of Robert the Bruce in Scottish history tells that as he watches a spider while hiding in a cave, he learns what he must do to save his people. As the narrator watches the spider in the first stanza of this poem, he also learns a lesson. What is the lesson that the narrator learns?

- 3. In the second stanza, the poet refers to "my Soul". Readers present different opinions about what this soul refers to. Some believe that Whitman is referring to Abraham Lincoln, the assassinated American President whom he greatly admired. Others believe it may be a woman whom he loved who has since died. Still others believe that he is referring to a part of himself, his own soul. In groups of three or four, explain why each of these three opinions may be a valid interpretation of the poem.

- 4. Watching an animal can cause a person to think about life. Native Canadian and American peoples believe that human beings can learn a great deal from the animals, and so they revere the animals. Write a poem or a paragraph in which you learn a valuable lesson about life from watching an animal.

PORTRAIT OF WILLIAM BLAKE

                   N1-163

WILLIAM BLAKE

William Blake gained his reputation as both a poet and an artist. He was born in London, England, in 1757, and was largely self-trained. By age twelve he was already writing poetry. At age fourteen, he became an apprentice to an engraver, a job which he followed throughout his life, by creating engraved pictures to illustrate books.

Blake's first book of poetry, *Poetical Sketches*, published in 1783, contains poems which he wrote before he reached the age of twenty-one. Most of his books were not published through the normal channels; instead, he created his own editions in small book format, illustrated by his original engravings. In *The Songs of Innocence*, published in 1789, and *The Songs of Experience*, published in 1794, he explored his relationship with God and with Jesus Christ, from the widely different points of view of an innocent child and a cynical, mature man. In later life, he resolved these contrasting perspectives by believing that innocence must pass through the world of experience before reaching a higher, third level.

His most famous poem is "Jerusalem", which he illustrated with both engravings and water colours. The book was published in 1820. The poem has been set to music and is often sung today in churches. It is a particularly popular hymn in Great Britain.

Blake claimed to see religious visions, even as a boy, and it is these visions which are captured in both his poetry and his engravings. Some labelled him as "insane", yet others saw his genius. His poetry was not widely circulated during his lifetime, and so he had little influence on his contemporaries. He truly characterized the spirit of the new Romantic movement, but it was left to poets such as William Wordsworth and Samuel Taylor Coleridge to proclaim the Romantic spirit; it is doubtful whether Wordsworth or Coleridge even read any of Blake's poems. Blake died in poverty in 1827, and was largely unknown at his death. By the end of the nineteenth century, however, his works were widely read and his genius was acknowledged.

In "Auguries of Innocence", written about 1800, William Blake's vision is made clear to all readers:
> To see a world in a grain of sand
> And a heaven in a wild flower,
> Hold infinity in the palm of your hand
> And eternity in an hour.

     N1-163

WILLIAM BLAKE: THE LAMB

Little Lamb, who made thee?
Dost thou know who made thee?
Gave thee life, and bid thee feed
By the stream, and o'er the mead;
Gave thee clothing of delight,
Softest clothing, woolly, bright;
Gave thee such a tender voice,
Making all the vales rejoice?
Little Lamb, who made thee?
Dost thou know who made thee?

Little Lamb, I'll tell thee,
Little Lamb, I'll tell thee:
He is callèd by thy name,
For he calls himself a Lamb.
He is meek, and he is mild;
He became a little child.
I a child, and thou a lamb.
We are callèd by His name.
Little Lamb, God bless thee!
Little Lamb, God bless thee!

WILLIAM BLAKE: THE TIGER

Tiger! Tiger! burning bright
In the forests of the night,
What immortal hand or eye
Could frame thy fearful symmetry?

In what distant deeps or skies
Burnt the fire of thine eyes?
On what wings dare he aspire?
What the hand dare seize the fire?

And what shoulder, and what art,
Could twist the sinews of thy heart,
And when thy heart began to beat,
What dread hand? and what dread feet?

What the hammer? what the chain?
In what furnace was thy brain?
What the anvil? what dread grasp
Dare its deadly terrors clasp?

When the stars threw down their spears,
And water'd heaven with their tears,
Did he smile his work to see?
Did he who made the Lamb make thee?

Tiger! Tiger! burning bright
In the forests of the night,
What immortal hand or eye,
Dare frame thy fearful symmetry?

N1-163

ACTIVITIES ON BLAKE'S POETRY

- 1. Look up the meaning of each of the following words:
    - mead
    - vales
    - meek
    - immortal
    - symmetry
    - aspire
    - sinews
    - dread
    - anvil.

- 2. "The Lamb" is taken from Blake's *The Songs of Innocence*. This anthology of poetry sees the world from the innocent perspective of the child; in this world, evil does not exist because everything is good. "The Tiger" comes from *The Songs of Experience*. The poems in this second book describe the world from the point of view of the mature, often cynical, man; all is evil in these poems, including humanity and even God. Both "The Lamb" and "The Tiger" ask the same question: Who made you? And the answer is God--an all-loving God in the first poem and a God who creates evil in the second poem. In groups of three or four, show that the lamb is the symbol of an all-loving world and that the tiger symbolizes evil. Explain what each poem says about the nature of God.

- 3. In the lines, "When the stars threw down their spears,/And water'd heaven with their tears", Blake is referring to the battle in heaven between God and the angels led by Lucifer, the Devil. What figure of speech is contained in these lines? Explain the comparison which Blake has used. Show that this is a particularly effective use of this figure of speech.

- 4. "The Tiger" compares the creation of the tiger (representing evil) with a creation made of metal in a forge. What words show this comparison? Explain why this is a particularly good example of a metaphor.

PORTRAIT OF DUNCAN CAMPBELL SCOTT

                             N1-163

DUNCAN CAMPBELL SCOTT

Duncan Campbell Scott is one a group of four poets who did their major writing after the Confederation of Canada was formed in 1867. For this reason, they are called the "Confederation Poets". The other three are Sir Charles G.D. Roberts (1860-1943), Bliss Carman (1861-1929) and Archibald Lampman (1861-1899). Together, these four poets produced the first poems of the Dominion of Canada.

Duncan Campbell Scott was born in Ottawa in 1862, of Scottish and English parentage. His father was a Methodist minister and Scott was educated at Stanstead College. From 1879 until 1932, Scott worked in the Department of Indian Affairs, eventually becoming its Director. He died in 1947.

Scott published eight volumes of poems, the first in 1893. As Director of the Department of Indian Affairs, Scott travelled extensively into the more remote parts of Canada and learned a great deal about the lives and legends of native peoples. He came to know native Canadians, but seemingly as an outsider; his poetry shows a sympathy but not a great deal of understanding, as if he were an observer rather than a participant. His poems show human beings in conflict with nature (a typical theme in Canadian literature); out of the conflict emerges a peace or serenity.

This same theme exists throughout twentieth century Canadian poetry, but later poets are not as naive in their writing: Often human beings are destroyed by nature; there is not peace or serenity. Students would gain a great deal of insight from reading some of the following Canadian poems:
- Earle Birney, "David"
- Margaret Atwood, "Progressive Insanities of a Pioneer"
- A.J.M. Smith, "The Lonely Land".

Not only was this theme important in poetry; painters also developed it in their art, particularly painters belonging to the Group of Seven. An excellent field trip would be to the McMichael Gallery in Kleinburg, Ontario, which has a magnificent collection of Group of Seven paintings. Students would enjoy making connections between Canadian poetry and the paintings of Lauren Harris, Frank Carmichael, Tom Thompson (not an actual member of the group, although influential in its founding) and others.

DUNCAN CAMPBELL SCOTT: THE FORSAKEN

Once in the winter
Out on a lake
In the heart of the north-land
Far from the Fort
And far from the hunters,
A Chippewa woman
With her sick baby,
Crouched in the last hours
Of a great storm.
Frozen and hungry,
She fished through the ice
With a line of the twisted
Bark of the cedar,
And a rabbit-bone hook
Polished and barbed;
Fished with the bare hook
All through the wild day,
Fished and caught nothing;
While the young chieftain
Tugged at her breasts,
Or slept in the lacings
Of the warm *tikanagan*.
All the lake-surface
Streamed with the hissing
Of millions of iceflakes
Hurled by the wind;
Behind her the round
Of a lonely island
Roared like a fire
With the voice of the storm
In the deeps of the cedars.
Valiant, unshaken,
She took of her own flesh,
Baited the fish-hook,
Drew in a grey-trout,

Drew in his fellows,
Heaped them beside her,
Dead in the snow.
Valiant, unshaken,
She faced the long distance,
Wolf-haunted and lonely,
Sure of her goal
And the life of her dear one:
Tramped for two days,
On the third in the morning,
Saw the strong bulk
Of the Fort by the river,
Saw the wood-smoke
Hang soft in the spruces,
Heard the keen yelp
Of the ravenous huskies
Fighting for whitefish:
Then she had rest.

Years and years after,
When she was old and withered,
When her son was an old man
And his children filled with vigour,
They came in their northern tour on the verge of winter,
To an island in a lonely lake.
There one night they camped, and on the morrow
Gathered their kettles and birch-bark,
Their rabbit-skin robes and their mink-traps,
Launched their canoes and slunk away through the islands,
Left her alone forever,
Without a word of farewell,
Because she was old and useless,
Like a paddle broken and warped,
Or a pole that was splintered.
Then, without a sigh,

Valiant, unshaken,
She smoothed her dark locks under her kerchief,
Composed her shawl in state,
Then folded her hands ridged with sinews and corded with veins,
Folded them across her breasts spent with the nourishing of children,
Gazed at the sky past the tops of the cedars,
Saw two spangled nights arise out of the twilight,
Saw two days go by filled with the tranquil sunshine,
Saw, without pain, or dread, or even a moment of longing:
Then on the third great night there came thronging and thronging
Millions of snowflakes out of a windless cloud;
They covered her close with a beautiful crystal shroud,
Covered her deep and silent.
But in the frost of the dawn,
Up from the life below,
Rose a column of breath
Through a tiny cleft in the snow,
Fragile, delicately drawn,
Wavering with its own weakness,
In the wilderness a sign of the spirit
Persisting still in the sight of the sun
Till day was done.
Then all light was gathered up by the hand of God and hid in His breast,
Then there was born a silence deeper than silence,
Then she had rest.

ACTIVITIES ON "THE FORSAKEN"

- 1. Explain the meaning of each of the following words:
  - crouched
  - tikanagan
  - bulk
  - ravenous
  - verge
  - spangled
  - thronging
  - shroud
  - wavering.

- 2. As Director of the Department of Indian Affairs, Duncan Campbell Scott supervised many aspects of the lives of Native Peoples. It is questionable, however, that he ever understood the point of view of the Native Peoples; he seemed always to see them from a detached, white man's perspective, and he seemed to evaluate them according to his own standards. For that reason, his poetry may be seen as perpetuating the stereotypes of North American Indians. What words, phrases or ideas in this poem only show the stereotypes?

- 3. Make a list of words which show the noble and unselfish nature of the Chippewa woman.

- 4. Hollywood movies have contributed greatly to advancing a stereotype of Native Peoples. What are the stereotypes presented in Westerns of the 1940s and 1950s, such as some of the John Wayne movies and the television series, *The Lone Ranger*. Make a list of movies which show Native Peoples as real human beings grappling with problems which threaten their existence. Explain clearly how each movie is able to break the earlier stereotypes.

PORTRAIT OF WILLIAM HENRY DRUMMOND

     N1-163

WILLIAM HENRY DRUMMOND

William Henry Drummond was born in Ireland in 1854 and, while he was still a young boy, emigrated to Canada with his family. His family settled near Montreal, but his father died shortly after their arrival. Gradually he was able to work his way through high school and university before graduating with a degree in medicine in 1884. He practised medicine in the Eastern Townships of Quebec, along the St. Lawrence River, where he met the "habitants" who were to become the subjects of his poetry.

Drummond wrote poems in the habitant dialect, and his first book, *The Habitant*, was published in 1897. His Preface to this book shows his affection for the quaint life styles of the Habitants:

> Having lived practically all my life, side by side with the French-Canadian people, I have grown to admire and love them, and I have felt that while many of the English-speaking public know perhaps as well as myself the French-Canadian of the cities, yet they have had little opportunity of becoming acquainted with the habitant.

Drummond used the dialect of the habitant as if the habitant were speaking in English to a non-French-speaking audience.

Drummond became a very popular poet in his day and earned a good income from his writing. He went on to publish five more books of poetry in the next ten or eleven years. In 1907, he died of a cerebral hemorrhage while fighting a smallpox epidemic at Cobalt, Ontario, where he had mining interests.

In this era of "political correctness", Drummond, like Henry Wadsworth Longfellow and Duncan Campbell Scott, has come under attack for perpetuating stereotypes. In his own time, however, Drummond seems to have been well respected and well loved by the French-Canadian people who read his poems and the habitants about whom he wrote.

WILLIAM HENRY DRUMMOND: LEETLE BATEESE

You bad leetle boy, not moche you care
How busy you're kippin' your poor gran'père
Tryin' to stop you ev'ry day
Chasin' de hen aroun' de hay--
Why don't you geev dem a chance to lay?
Leetle Bateese!

Off on de fiel' you foller de plough
Den w'en you're tire you scare the cow
Sickin' de dog till dey jomp the wall
So de milk ain't good for not'ing at all--
An' you're only five an' a half dis fall,
Leetle Bateese!

Too sleepy for sayin' de prayer tonight?
Never min' I s'pose it'll be all right
Say dem tomorrow--ah! dere he go!
Fas' asleep in a minute or so--
An' he'll stay lak dat till de rooster crow,
Leetle Bateese!

Den wake us up right away toute suite
Lookin' for somet'ing more to eat,
Makin' me t'ink of dem long leg crane
Soon as dey swaller, dey start again,
I wonder your stomach don't get no pain,
Leetle Bateese!

But see heem now lyin' dere in bed,
Look at de arm onderneat' hees head;
If he grow lak dat till he's twenty year
I bet he'll be strong dan Louis Cyr
An' beat all de voyageurs leevin' here,
Leetle Bateese!

Jus' feel de muscle along hees back,
Won't geev heem moche bodder for carry pack
On de long portage, any size canoe,
Dere's not many t'ing dat boy won't do
For he's got double-joint on hees body too,
Leetle Bateese!

But leetle Bateese! please don't forget
We rader you're stayin' de small boy yet,
So chase de chicken an' mak' dem scare
An' do w'at you lak wit' your ole gran'père
For w'en you're beeg feller he won't be dere--
Leetle Bateese!

WILLIAM HENRY DRUMMOND: THE WRECK OF THE "JULIE PLANTE"

On wan dark night on Lac St. Pierre,
  De win' she blow, blow, blow,
An' de crew of de wood scow "Julie Plante"
  Got scar't an' run below--
For de win' she blow lake hurricane,
  Blimeby she blow some more,
An' de scow bus' up on Lac St. Pierre
  Wan arpent from de shore.

De captinne walk on de fronte deck,
  An' walk de hin' deck too--
He call de crew from up de hole,
  He call de cook also.
De cook she's name was Rosie,
  She come from Montreal,
Was chambre maid on lumber barge,
  On de Grande Lachine Canal.

De win' she blow from nor'-eas'-wes'--
  De sout' win' she blow too,
W'en Rosie cry, "Mon cher captinne,
  Mon cher, w'at I shall do?
Den de captinne t'row de big ankerre,
  But still de scow she dreef,
De crew he can't pass on de shore,
  Becos he los' hees skeef.

De night was dark lak wan black cat,
  De wave run high an' fas',
W'en de captinne tak' de Rosie girl
  An' tie her to de mas'.
Den he also tak' de life preserve,
  An' jomp off on de lak',
An' say, "Goodbye, ma Rosie dear,
  I go drown for you sak'."

Nex' morning very early
  'Bout ha'f-pas' two--t'ree--four--
De captinne--scow--an' de poor Rosie
  Was corpses on de shore,
For de win' she blow lak hurricane,
  Blimeby she blow some more,
An' de scow bus' up on Lac St. Piere,
  Wan arpent from de shore.

Now all good wood scow sailor man
  Tak' warning by dat storm
An' go an' marry some nice French girl
  An' leev on wan beeg farm.
De win' can blow lak hurricane
  An' s'pose she blow some more,
You can't get drown on Lac St. Pierre
  So long you stay on shore.

ACTIVITIES ON DRUMMOND'S POETRY

- 1. Drummond writes his poetry using the dialect which a French-Canadian "habitant" might use if he were telling a story in English to someone who does not understand French. He spells his words as they would be pronounced by the habitant. "Bateese", for example, is "Baptiste", a fairly common name in French Canada. Often his poems are easier to understand if they are read out loud. In groups of four or five, practise reading each poem out loud. Then present your reading to the class with each group member reading one or two stanzas.

- 2. **Pathos** is the arousing of feelings of pity or sadness in the reader. What line in "Leetle Bateese" creates pathos? Why does Drummond choose to create pathos at the end of a generally humorous poem?

- 3. Often the rhyme in Drummond's poems can help the reader to pronounce the dialect. In "The Wreck of the Julie Plante", for example, the word "Montreal" in the second stanza is pronounced the French way (More-Ray-Al, not Mont-Re-All) so it will rhyme with "Canal". What is the rhyme scheme Drummond uses in each poem?

- 4. Use the Internet to do some background research into some of the people and places which Drummond described in his poems at the turn of the century. Check the following:
  - Louis Cyr
  - the Voyageurs
  - Lac St. Pierre
  - Lachine Canal.

- 5. Write a poem or a story using dialect. You may use a regional accent (for example, a New York City Bronx accent or a Texas accent) or an accent from a non-English speaking country. Try to show the person using this accent in a sympathetic light; do not use the accent to make fun of anyone. Read your poem or story to the class.

PORTRAIT OF EMILY DICKINSON

71

EMILY DICKINSON

Emily Dickinson was born in Amherst, Massachusetts, in 1830, into a family which had lived in New England for eight generations. She had a very strict and intensely religious upbringing and was largely educated at home. When she was young, Dickinson apparently had a very disappointing experience in love, and from that point on, she rarely left her home, corresponding with the outside world mainly through letters.

Emily Dickinson was a very shy person and wrote her poetry for herself, not for publication. As a matter of fact, her poems were not published until four years after her death. They were found by her sister, Lavinia; many of the poems were scribbled on scraps of paper, on newspapers or on the backs of envelopes.

Dickinson's poems are highly personal but reflect upon universal themes, such as love, death and God. Much of her work derives from an observation of nature around her home in Amherst. She has an acute talent for using words for their various connotations and often uses near-rhymes (called **assonance**), such as "ring" and "sun". In addition, the lines of her poems are often fragments punctuated with dashes. These characteristics, the combination of her content and her style, produce an almost mystical quality to her verse, which makes her poetry quite different from that of her contemporary, Walt Whitman.

Dickinson died in 1886, known only to a few people. The publication of her works after her death, however, has made Emily Dickinson world famous. She is recognized today as one of the finest American poets.

EMILY DICKINSON: "A NARROW FELLOW IN THE GRASS"

A narrow fellow in the grass
Occasionally rides--
You may have met him--did you not--
His notice sudden is.

The grass divides as with a comb--
A spotted shaft is seen--
And then it closes at your feet
And opens farther on.

He likes a boggy acre,
A floor too cool for corn--
Yet when a child and barefoot--
I more than once at morn--

Have passed--I thought--a whip-lash
Unbraiding in the sun--
When stooping to secure it--
It wrinkled, and was gone--

Several of nature's people--
I know--and they know me;
I feel for them a transport
Of cordiality--

But never met this fellow--
Attended or alone--
Without a tighter breathing--
And zero at the bone.

EMILY DICKINSON: "I LIKE TO SEE IT LAP THE MILES"

I like to see it lap the Miles--
And lick the Valleys up--
And stop to feed itself at Tanks--
And then--prodigious step

Around a Pile of Mountains--
And supercilious peer
In Shanties--by the sides of Roads--
And then a Quarry pare

To fit its ribs and crawl between
Complaining all the while
In horrid--hooting stanza--
Then chase itself down Hill--

And neigh like Boanerges--
Then--prompter than a Star
Stop--docile and omnipotent
At its own stable door--

Note: This is not a horse, although it is compared to a horse.

EMILY DICKINSON: "THE BRAIN IS WIDER THAN THE SKY"

The Brain--is wider than the Sky--
For--put them side by side--
The one the other will contain
With ease--and You--beside--

The Brain is deeper than the sea--
For--hold them--Blue to Blue--
The one the other will absorb--
As Sponges--Buckets--do

The Brain is just the weight of God--
For--Heft them--Pound for Pound--
And they will differ--if they do--
As Syllable from Sound--

ACTIVITIES ON DICKINSON'S POETRY

- 1. Dickinson did not write her work to be published and read by anyone else. Sometimes her poems appear like puzzles.
    - "A Narrow Fellow in the Grass" is easy to identify. What animal is Dickinson describing in this poem? Point out three phrases which provide clues to the animal.
    - "I Like to See It Lap the Miles" is a more difficult puzzle. Note that Dickinson compares "it" to a horse, but "it" is not a horse. Concentrate on the following clues to discover what "it" is: It crawls through a quarry which fits its ribs; it chases itself down hill; it hoots. What is it?

- 2. Explain what each of the following words means:
    - shaft
    - a whip-lash (not what can damage a person's neck)
    - cordiality
    - prodigious
    - supercilious
    - quarry
    - docile
    - omnipotent
    - heft.

- 3. In "The Brain Is Wider Than The Sky", Dickinson presents two contrasts and then a comparison. How is a brain wider than sky and deeper than sea? How is the brain like God? (Note that Dickinson does not provide a satisfactory answer to the second question; you will need to use your own imagination to answer it.)

- 4. Emily Dickinson uses imagery with ease. Find one good image in each of her poems and explain how this image helps to develop the theme of the poem.

ACTIVITIES FOR ESSAY WRITING AND DISCUSSION

The following will make good essay topics or topics for discussion and debate. The teacher may also use them for seminars presented by groups of three or four students.

- 1. Several of the poems in this unit deal with heroism. Compare and contrast the views of heroism shown in the following poems. Which poem comes closest to expressing your view of what it means to be a hero?
  - "Sir Patrick Spens"
  - "The Village Blacksmith"
  - "The Charge of the Light Brigade"
  - "Lochinvar"
  - "The Forsaken"
  - "The Wreck of the Julie Plante".

- 2. The Romantic Woman is a constant theme in poetry. Sometimes women are depicted as the modern counterparts of Eve, who tempt men and lead them to their downfalls; sometimes women are treated as sex objects. Compare and contrast the treatment of women in the following poems:
  - "The Daemon Lover"
  - "Get Up and Bar the Door"
  - "Sonnet XVIII"
  - "La Belle Dame Sans Merci"
  - "The Wreck of the Julie Plante".

- 3. Compare and contrast the treatment of native peoples in "Hiawatha's Childhood" and "The Forsaken". Which of the poets gives the more realistic view of native peoples? Find a poem written by a contemporary North American Indian to compare or to contrast to the two nineteenth century poems written by white males.

ACTIVITIES FOR ESSAY WRITING AND DISCUSSION (Continued)

- 4. Several of the poems in this unit tell stories. Show what techniques each poet has used to create an interesting story in four of:
  - "The Daemon Lover"
  - "Sir Patrick Spens"
  - "The Charge of the Light Brigade"
  - "Lochinvar"
  - "The Owl and the Pussycat"
  - "The Forsaken"
  - "The Wreck of the Julie Plante".

- 5. Compare and contrast the attitude towards nature presented in four of the following poems:
  - The Witches from Macbeth
  - "La Belle Dame Sans Merci"
  - "Hiawatha's Childhood"
  - "A Narrow Fellow In The Grass"
  - "A Noiseless Patient Spider"
  - "The Forsaken"
  - "Leetle Bateese"
  - "The Wreck of the Julie Plante".

- 6. Which poet makes the best use of imagery to convey the message of the poem? Defend your answer with specific examples of imagery.

- 7. Which poet uses language to the best advantage to develop the theme of the poem? Support your answer with examples of effective diction.

- 8. Poetry is the use of images to convey a theme. List five possible themes for poems. Then choose two of these themes; for each one, list five possible images which may express that theme. Now choose one of these themes and write a poem using at least three of the five images you have selected for it.

ACTIVITIES (Continued)

WORD SEARCH

Search for the names of the following poets:

Shakespeare	Keats
Longfellow	Tennyson
Scott	Lear
Whitman	Blake
Drummond	Dickinson.

L	A	W	D	I	C	K	I	N	S	O	N
O	S	W	S	X	D	F	G	I	C	F	E
N	R	H	P	B	A	U	S	L	O	S	D
G	E	I	A	J	L	D	E	A	T	D	R
F	A	T	D	K	E	A	T	S	T	C	U
E	B	M	K	R	E	D	K	C	M	W	M
L	H	A	S	P	D	S	O	E	C	N	M
L	W	N	S	G	O	A	P	B	Y	T	O
O	T	Q	N	Z	U	S	A	E	N	E	N
W	T	E	N	N	Y	S	O	N	A	W	D
Y	O	U	H	M	S	U	D	E	I	R	N
A	P	P	Y	L	E	A	R	D	A	V	E

ACTIVITIES (Continued)

WORD SEARCH ANSWERS

Search for the names of the following poets:

Shakespeare	Keats
Longfellow	Tennyson
Scott	Lear
Whitman	Blake
Drummond	Dickinson.

L			D	I	C	K	I	N	S	O	N
O	S	W							C		
N		H		B					O		D
G		I	A		L				T		R
F		T		K	E	A	T	S	T		U
E		M			E		K				M
L		A			S			E			M
L		N				P					O
O							E				N
W	T	E	N	N	Y	S	O	N	A		D
										R	
			L	E	A	R					E

Publication Listing